Still searching

Nicole Marie Raymond

Presentation by *BookLeaf Publishing*

Web: www.bookleafpub.com

E-mail: info@bookleafpub.com

ISBN: 9789358737462

First edition 2023

To jtr

for loving me anyway

ACKNOWLEDGEMENT

To all the threads in the fabric of my life... don't we all make a wonderful weave?

PREFACE

To all the versions of me: past, present, and future.

May these poems be a light aling the path.

fiction

Running to or running from?
 Intelligence or ignorance?

Duplicity or simplicity?

Am I just a contradiction? a doormat? a joke?

A scared, abandoned and lonely child
behind a stone wall with pretty windows

but

They've huffed and they've puffed
and ...
I've clawed the walls down for them.

still they don't see me

connection

Tipped by toxicity
Unavoidable in a connected world

To disconnect equals what: death?
dismemberment? despair?

or
would it be a blessing to be an individual in a
sea of conformity...
drifting amongst the waves...
surfing the turbulence of mass hysteria?

truth

3

To discover the truth
  you have to face it.

  but who will ever make you?
   who would ever want to?

  what happens when there are no more
questions?

  ... the duality of my soul.

The mind

I'm on a forced march through my mind.
 There are many dark tunnels here.
 Long, still pools--falsely deep, reflective only
through my dark lenses

 A small glimpse of color and light
 A quick detour into whimsy.

 Feet and heart want calmer paths.
 The lungs deep, cleansing breath,
But the mind-the mind...
 the mind would keep us wandering

Fibonacci's Guide Posts

5

Life is a series of spirals.
 We turn each bend to live the same
experience.(but we have changed)
 The guide post's blazes now harder to see, as the
spiral circles wide.
 (still they are there to mark the way)
 It's all the same.

Labels

6

what do you call the spaces in between the lessons?

wisdom. luck. life. living.

rest.

You can only carry so much

Strength,
you can only carry so much.
Empathy,
you can only carry so much.
Guilt,
you can only carry so much.
Sadness,
you can only carry so much.
Pride,
you can only carry so much.
Fear,
you can only carry so much.
Greed,
you can only carry so much.

While waiting

Almost everything we see and learn in this life
creates the expectation of fitting in it's
prescribed and neat space.

Pictures in frames, rooms in boxes, books in
binding.

We color inside the lines and tidy up the edges.

Yet
We are not finite. Our edges are not straight.
We're clipped and shorn to fit just so,
perhaps losing the best parts--
the tendrils that are reaching
the branches about to grab the light

Life cannot be contained

Learn this, please

9

The brain gets in the way

Overthinking is a dangerous disease

you see me and you stay

You see me and you stay

 you laugh in the right spots, you give me your shoulder

 you laugh in the right spots, you chase the demons

you show me yours. I show you mine.

we laugh in the right spots and we stay

you see me and you stay

it finds a way

if you don't let it out, it finds a way

it seeps, it weeps,

it belches, it creaks.

it cracks lines in your face

why do you choke it down when it tries to
escape?

we all must feel pain

so feel,

it only hurts once if you let it go.

the girl who followed the cat

i don't remember her much, the girl who
followed the cat on an adventure through the
woods,

she must have been brave and sure, full of
wonder.

i don't think all of her came back.

she was tethered and fed less of a lead.

one day, Ordinary slapped it's collar on.

i don't think she liked it. it chafed and choked.

she wore it for almost a lifetime.

and then she remembered,
she's the girl who followed the cat

and just like that, it's gone.

Poem Thirteen

13

The only real thing I have of me.

October 13: fact

the rest is what I am told. what I can grab and
what I can hold.
what sticks.
what I earned, what I have learned.

but thirteen is the piece of me that is sure. it's
my security blanket it's my mask its my
umbrella its my bandage.

this little bit of truly me: 13.

Loss

14

The fourteenth was the last day, but the loss was stretched long and we didn't even know it had begun.

Sitting by the window, holding your hand.

All four seasons showed up in those hours,

The red leaves blazed and were letting go.

I knew you would stay to the end.

The last leaf fell.

You were gone.

love

15

I knew almost at once how lucky I'd be.

First hooded and dark in the corner,
my hero

There was a promise in your crooked grin

Look where we have been

Sealed the promise in the sand

Created life, protected life

Now to live a life.... love

Little Love

a dream and a miracle

guarded and nurtured

held and hugged

breathed and loved

a joy and a blessing

the future

pieces

17

all the pieces scattered
 i could not find them all
 i kept going back to see if you kept some

 i made a new one, but i used the wrong glue and
i lost more pieces too

 secretly, I designed another made to last this
time, because I knew the glue to hold together
had to be just mine, that is the strongest kind

letting go

a snake sheds, a bird molts,
 but what can a person do?

 how do you let go of deadness which you
always carry with you...

 can you slough if it off in whispers to be carried
on the wind...

 or do you need to scream it out and make it live
again

 or are tears the best way to evaporate the pain

 is acknowledgement of all that's true what
makes you whole again?

the things that stick

19

it's funny to me the things that stick

fantasy, daydream, dread

it's funny to me how things just stick and make
camp in my head

I seem to give free parking to the things that
hurt the most, but for kindness, smiles and
compliments I am a measured host.

to doubt and to question
I serve the choicest cuts

but to things that sound like compliments, I
keep the windows shut

silly it is to live this way
I think it makes me sick
to constantly keep choking down those
things that seem to stick

forward

I had been there for a while
 afraid to make that step

 the one that moved me forward to a place I'd
never been

 It meant I'd leave behind the comforts of my
past, even though all the comforts were buried
beneath masks

 but then one day, I'd had it
 I was tired of myself
 I made the leap, before I could
 retract what I would do

 I floundered, and I pondered and I learned now
how to move

 forward

just breathe

just breathe ...

    in those moments when you're happy
    in those moments full of grief
    in those moments you rejoice outside
    in those moments before sleep

just breathe...
when you wake up in the morning
when you hold your lover's hand
when you stare out at the ocean
with feet buried in the sand

just breathe...
when you hear a child's laughter
when you wipe a child's tear

when you hug your family closer
when you celebrate the years

when you need to find the courage
when you need to feel the pain
when you see the truth before you
when you look back once again

just breathe
when you find the joy, the reason
when one and one make two,
when everything is working
when you know that you are you